# PRAYERS AND PROMISES FOR

*Men*

*A Topical Devotional*

# PRAYERS AND PROMISES FOR

*Men*

ISBN 1-58334-198-6

*The quoted ideas expressed in this book (but not scripture verses) are not, in all cases, exact quotations, as some have been edited for clarity and brevity. In all cases, the author has attempted to maintain the speaker's original intent. In some cases, quoted material for this book was obtained from secondary sources, primarily print media. While every effort was made to ensure the accuracy of these sources, the accuracy cannot be guaranteed. For additions, deletions, corrections or clarifications in future editions of this text, please write BRIGHTON BOOKS.*

Scripture taken from the HOLY BIBLE, NEW INTERNATIONAL VERSION ©. NIV ©. Copyright © 1973, 1978, 1984, by International Bible Society. Used by permission of Zondervan Publishing House. All rights reserved.

Scripture taken from *THE MESSAGE*. Copyright © 1993, 1994,1995,1996. Used by permission of NavPress Publishing Group.

Scripture quotations marked (NLT) are taken from The Holy Bible, New Living Translation, Copyright © 1996. Used by permission of Tyndale House Publishers, Incorporated, Wheaton, Illinois 60189. All rights reserved.

Scripture quotations are taken from the Holman Christian Standard Bible™, Copyright © 1999, 2000, 2001 by Holman Bible Publishers, used by permission.

Scripture taken from the NEW AMERICAN STANDARD BIBLE®, Copyright © 1960, 1962, 1963, 1968, 1971, 1972, 1973, 1975, 1977, 1995 by The Lockman Foundation. Used by permission.

Printed in the United States of America
Cover Design: Holli Conger
Page Layout: Bart Dawson

1 2 3 4 5 6 7 8 9 10 • 03 04 05 06 07 08 09 10

# Table of Contents

# INTRODUCTION

This morning and every morning, the sun rises upon a world filled with God's presence and His love. As believing Christians, we have so many reasons to celebrate: God is in His heaven, His love is everlasting, and we, His children, are blessed beyond measure. Yet, on some days we may find ourselves distracted by the inevitable demands and frustrations of everyday life. This little book is intended to redirect our thoughts—and our days—toward God.

The fabric of daily life is woven together with the threads of habit, and no habit is more important than that of consistent prayer and daily devotion to our Creator. This text contains a collection of brief devotional readings arranged by topic. Each two-page chapter contains Bible verses, a devotional reading, quotations from noted Christian thinkers, and a prayer. Each chapter is intended to remind you of God's love, of His Son, and of His promises.

God loves you more than you can fathom, and He will give you comfort and protection *if* you turn your mind and your heart to Him. So turn to Him today and every day. When you do, you will discover that the Lord is indeed your Shepherd and that you are protected now and throughout eternity.

# ABUNDANCE

I am come that they might have life, and
that they might have it more abundantly.
*John 10:10 KJV*

The 10th chapter of John tells us that Christ came to earth so that our lives might be filled with abundance. But what, exactly, did Jesus mean when He promised "life…more abundantly"? Was He referring to material possessions or financial wealth? Hardly. Jesus offers a different kind of abundance: a spiritual richness that extends beyond the temporal boundaries of this world.

Is material abundance part of God's plan for our lives? Perhaps. But in every circumstance of life, during times of wealth or times of want, God will provide us what we need *if* we trust Him (Matthew 6). May we, as believers, claim the riches of Christ Jesus every day that we live, and may we share His blessings with all who cross our paths.

God loves you and wants you to experience
peace and life—abundant and eternal.
*Billy Graham*

# Thoughts on Spiritual Abundance

We honor God by asking for great things when
they are a part of His promise. We dishonor Him
and cheat ourselves when we ask for molehills
where He has promised mountains.

*Vance Havner*

Ask and it will be given to you;
seek and you will find; knock and the door will
be opened to you. For everyone who asks receives;
he who seeks finds; and to him who knocks,
the door will be opened.

*Matthew 7:7-8 NIV*

Father, thank You for the joyful, abundant life
that is mine through Christ Jesus. Guide me
according to Your will, and help me to be a worthy
servant through all that I say and do. Give me
courage, Lord, to claim the spiritual riches that
You have promised, and lead me according to
Your plan for my life, today and always.

—Amen—

# ADVERSITY

For whatsoever is born of God
overcometh the world….

*1 John 5:4 KJV*

All of us face times of adversity. On occasion, we all must endure the disappointments and tragedies that befall believers and nonbelievers alike. The reassuring words of 1 John 5:4 remind us that when we accept God's grace we overcome the passing hardships of this world by relying upon His strength, His love, and His promise of eternal life.

When we face the inevitable difficulties of life here on earth, God stands ready to protect us. Our responsibility, of course, is to ask Him for protection. When we call upon Him in heartfelt prayer, He will answer—in His own time and according to His own plan—and He will heal us. And while we are waiting for God's plans to unfold and for His healing touch to restore us, we can be comforted in the knowledge that our Creator can overcome any obstacle, even if we cannot. Let us take God at His word, and let us trust Him.

Some virtues cannot be produced
in us without affliction.

*C. H. Spurgeon*

# Trusting God in Difficult Times

When times are tough,
the Lord is our only security.
*Charles Swindoll*


Here, then, is the secret of endurance when
the going is tough: God is producing a harvest in
our lives. He wants the "fruit of the Spirit" to grow
(Galatians 5:22-23), and the only way He can
do it is through trials and troubles.
*Warren Wiersbe*


In my distress I called upon the LORD and
cried unto my God: he heard my voice....
*Psalm 18:6 KJV*


Dear Heavenly Father, when I am troubled,
You heal me. When I am afraid, You protect me.
When I am discouraged, You lift me up. You are
my unending source of strength, Lord; let me turn
to You when I am weak. In times of adversity,
let me trust Your plan and Your will for my life.
And whatever my circumstances, Lord, let me
always give the thanks and the glory to You.
—Amen—

# ANGER

I want men everywhere to lift up holy hands
in prayer, without anger or disputing.
*1 Timothy 2:8 NIV*

Sometimes, anger is appropriate. Even Jesus
became angry when confronted with the
moneychangers in the temple. On occasion, you, like
Jesus, will confront evil, and when you do, you may
respond as He did: vigorously and without reser-
vation. But, more often than not, your frustrations
will be of the more mundane variety.

As long as you live here on earth, you will face
countless opportunities to lose your temper over
small, relatively insignificant events: a traffic jam, a
spilled cup of coffee, an inconsiderate comment, a
broken promise. When you are tempted to lose your
temper over the minor inconveniences of life, don't.
Turn away from anger, hatred, bitterness, and regret.
Turn instead to God.

When you strike out in anger, you may miss the
other person, but you will always hit yourself.
*Jim Gallery*

# THOUGHTS ABOUT ANGER

What is hatred, after all, other than anger that was
allowed to remain, that has become ingrained and
deep-rooted? What was anger when it was fresh
becomes hatred when it is aged.

*St. Augustine*

Refrain from anger and turn from wrath;
do not fret—it leads only to evil.

*Psalm 37:8 NIV*

Lord, sometimes, I am quick to anger and slow
to forgive. But I know, Lord, that You seek
abundance and peace for my life. Forgiveness is
Your commandment; empower me to follow the
example of Your Son Jesus who forgave His
persecutors. As I turn away from anger, I claim
the peace that You intend for my life.

—Amen—

# ATTITUDE

Finally, brethren, whatever is true, whatever is
honorable, whatever is right, whatever is pure,
whatever is lovely, whatever is of good repute,
if there is any excellence and if anything worthy
of praise, dwell on these things.

*Philippians 4:8 NASB*

How will you direct your thoughts today? Will you obey the words of Philippians 4:8 by dwelling upon those things that are honorable, true, and worthy of praise? Or will you allow your thoughts to be hijacked by the negativity that seems to dominate our troubled world. Are you fearful, angry, bored, or worried? Are you so preoccupied with the concerns of this day that you fail to thank God for the promise of eternity? Are you confused, bitter, or pessimistic? If so, God wants to have a little talk with you.

God intends that you experience joy and abundance, but He will not force His joy upon you; you must claim it for yourself. So, today and every day hereafter, celebrate this life that God has given you by focusing your thoughts and your energies upon "whatever is of good repute." Today, count your blessings instead of your hardships. And thank the Giver of all things good for gifts that are simply too numerous to count.

# GUARDING OUR THOUGHTS

Often, attitude is the only difference
between success and failure.
*John Maxwell*


A positive attitude will have positive results
because attitudes are contagious.
*Zig Ziglar*


Therefore, since Christ suffered in his body,
arm yourselves also with the same attitude,
because he who has suffered in his body is done
with sin. As a result, he does not live the rest
of his earthly life for evil human desires,
but rather for the will of God.
*1 Peter 4:1-2 NIV*

Lord, I pray for an attitude that is Christlike.
Whatever the circumstances I face, whether good
or bad, triumphal or tragic, may my response
reflect a God-honoring, Christlike attitude
of optimism, faith, and love for You.
—Amen—

# BEHAVIOR

Therefore, since we have this ministry, as we
received mercy, we do not lose heart, but we have
renounced the things hidden because of shame,
not walking in craftiness or adulterating
the word of God, but by the manifestation
of truth commending ourselves to every man's
conscience in the sight of God.

*2 Corinthians 4:1-2 NASB*

Life is a series of decisions and choices. Each
day, we make countless decisions that can
bring us closer to God…or not. When we live
according to God's commandments, we earn for
ourselves the abundance and peace that He intends
for our lives. But, when we turn our backs upon God
by disobeying Him, we bring needless suffering upon
ourselves and our families.

Do you seek God's peace and His blessings? Then
obey Him. When you're faced with a difficult choice
or a powerful temptation, seek God's counsel and
trust the counsel He gives. Invite God into your heart
and live according to His commandments. When
you do, you will be blessed today and tomorrow and
forever.

# Living in Accordance with Our Beliefs

Resolved: never to do anything which I should
be afraid to do if it were the last hour of my life.

*Jonathan Edwards*

Order your soul; reduce your wants; associate
in Christian community; obey the laws;
trust in Providence.

*St. Augustine*

Discipline yourself for the purpose of godliness.

*1 Timothy 4:7 NASB*

—————

Dear Lord, there is a right way and a wrong way
to live. Let me live according to Your rules, not
the world's rules. Your path is right for me, God;
let me follow it every day of my life.

—Amen—

# CELEBRATION

Rejoice in the Lord always.
I will say it again: Rejoice!
*Philippians 4:4 HCSB*

Oswald Chambers correctly observed, "Joy is the great note all throughout the Bible." But, even the most dedicated Christians can, on occasion, forget to celebrate each day for what it is: a priceless gift from God.

Today, let us celebrate life as God intended. Today, let us share the good news of Jesus Christ. Today, let us put smiles on our faces, kind words on our lips, and songs in our hearts. Let us be generous with our praise and free with our encouragement. And then, when we have celebrated life to the full, let us invite others to do likewise. After all, this is God's day, and He has given us clear instructions for its use. We are commanded to rejoice and be glad. So, with no further ado, let the celebration begin....

If his presence does not cheer you, surely heaven itself would not make you glad; for what is heaven but the full enjoyment of his love?
*C. H. Spurgeon*

# CELEBRATING GOD'S GIFTS

If our hearts have been attuned to God through
an abiding faith in Christ, the result will be
joyous optimism and good cheer.

*Billy Graham*


In commanding us to glorify Him,
God is inviting us to enjoy Him.

*C. S. Lewis*


I will thank you, LORD, with all my heart;
I will tell of all the marvelous things you have
done. I will be filled with joy because of you.
I will sing praises to your name, O Most High.

*Psalm 9:1-2 NLT*

✤

Lord God, You have given me so many reasons to
celebrate. The heavens proclaim Your handiwork,
and every star in the sky tells of Your power. You
sent Your Son to die for my sins, and You gave me
the gift of eternal life. Let me be mindful of all my
blessings, and let me celebrate You and Your
marvelous creation. Today is Your gift to me, Lord.
Let me use it to Your glory.

—Amen—

# CHRIST'S LOVE

For I am convinced that neither death, nor life,
nor angels, nor principalities, nor things present,
nor things to come, nor powers, nor height,
nor depth, nor any other created thing,
will be able to separate us from the love of God,
which is in Christ Jesus our Lord.

*Romans 8:38-39 NASB*

What does the love of Christ mean to His believers? It changes everything. His love is perfect and steadfast. Even though we are fallible, and wayward, the Good Shepherd cares for us still.

Even though we have fallen far short of the Father's commandments, Christ loves us with a power and depth that are beyond our understanding. And, as we accept Christ's love and walk in Christ's footsteps, our lives bear testimony to His power and to His grace. Yes, Christ's love changes everything; may we invite Him into our hearts so it can then change everything in us.

Jesus is all compassion. He never betrays us.

*Catherine Marshall*

# Jesus Is . . .

Christ reigns in his church as shepherd-king.
He has supremacy, but it is the superiority of a wise
and tender shepherd over his needy and loving
flock. He commands and receives obedience,
but it is willing obedience of well-cared-for sheep,
offered joyfully to their beloved Shepherd,
whose voice they know so well. He rules by the
force of love and the energy of goodness.

*C. H. Spurgeon*

There is a God-shaped hole in every man
that only God can fill.

*St. Augustine*

But God commendeth his love toward us, in that,
while we were yet sinners, Christ died for us.

*Romans 5:8 KJV*

Dear Jesus, I am humbled by Your love and mercy.
You went to Calvary so that I might have eternal
life. Thank You, Jesus, for Your priceless gift,
and for Your love. You loved me first, Lord,
and I will return Your love today and forever.
—Amen—

# THE CHURCH

Take heed therefore unto yourselves, and to all
the flock, over the which the Holy Ghost hath
made you overseers, to feed the church of God.

*Acts 20:28 KJV*

In the Book of Acts, Luke reminds us to "feed
the church of God." As Christians who have
been saved by a loving, compassionate Creator, we
are compelled not only to worship Him in our hearts
but also to worship Him in the presence of fellow
believers. The church belongs to God; it is His just
as certainly as we are His. When we help build God's
church, we bear witness to the changes that He has
made in our lives.

Today and every day, let us worship God with
grateful hearts and helping hands as we support the
church that He has created. Let us witness to our
friends, to our families, and to the world. When we
do so, we bless others and we are blessed by the One
who sent His Son to die so that we might have
eternal life.

And how can we improve the church?
Simply and only by improving ourselves.

*A. W. Tozer*

# THOUGHTS ON GOD'S CHURCH

All too often, the church holds up a mirror
reflecting back the society around it, rather than
a different way.

*Philip Yancey*

Every time a new person comes to God, every time
someone's gifts find expression in the fellowship of
believers, every time a family in need is surrounded
by the caring church, the truth is affirmed anew:
the Church triumphant is alive and well!

*Gloria Gaither*

For where two or three come together
in my name, there am I with them.

*Matthew 18:20 NIV*

Lord, wherever it is that we worship,
You are there. Let me support Your church,
let me help build Your church, and let me
remember that church is not only a place;
it is also a state of mind and a state of grace.
—Amen—

# COURAGE

Don't be afraid, for I am with you.
Do not be dismayed for I am your God.
I will strengthen you. I will help you.
I will uphold you with my victorious right hand.

*Isaiah 41:10 NLT*

I n moments of triumph, we find it easy to be bold. But, when the storm clouds of life form overhead and we find ourselves in the dark valley of despair, our faith is stretched, sometimes to the breaking point. As Christians, we can be comforted: wherever we find ourselves, whether at the top of the mountain or the depths of the valley, God is there, and because He cares for us, we can live courageously.

The next time you find your courage tested to the limit, remember that God is as near as your next breath, and remember that He offers salvation to His children. He is your shield and your strength; He is your protector and your deliverer. Call upon Him in your hour of need and then be comforted. Whatever your challenge, whatever your trouble, God can handle it. And will.

Take courage. We walk in the wilderness today and in the Promised Land tomorrow.

*D. L. Moody*

# Thoughts on Courage and Faith

Faith is stronger than fear.

*John Maxwell*

Are you fearful? First, bow your head and pray
for God's strength. Then, raise your head knowing
that, together, you and God can handle
whatever comes your way.

*Jim Gallery*

The LORD himself goes before you and will be
with you; he will never leave you nor forsake you.
Do not be afraid; do not be discouraged.

*Deuteronomy 31:8 NIV*

Lord, let me turn to You for courage
and for strength. When I am fearful, keep me
mindful of Your promises. When I am anxious,
let me turn my thoughts and prayers to
the priceless gift of Your Son. You are with me
always, Heavenly Father, and I will face
the challenges of this day with trust and
assurance in You.

—Amen—

# EVIL

A good man out of the good treasure of the heart
bringeth forth good things: and an evil man out
of the evil treasure bringeth forth evil things.

*Matthew 12:35 KJV*

This world is God's creation, and it contains the wonderful fruits of His handiwork. But, it also contains countless opportunities to stray from God's will. Temptations are everywhere, and the devil, it seems, never takes a day off. Our task, as believers, is to turn away from temptation and to place our lives squarely in the center of God's will.

In his letter to Jewish Christians, Peter offered a stern warning: "Your adversary, the devil, prowls around like a roaring lion, seeking someone to devour" (1 Peter 5:8 NASB). What was true in New Testament times is equally true in our own. Evil is indeed abroad in the world, and Satan continues to sow the seeds of destruction far and wide. As Christians we must earnestly wrap ourselves in the protection of God's Holy Word. When we do, we are secure.

We need not despair of any man so long as
he lives. For God deemed it better to bring good
out of evil than not to permit evil at all.

*St. Augustine*

# Resisting the Evils of This World

Of two evils, choose neither.
*C. H. Spurgeon*

There is nothing evil in matter itself. Evil lies
in the spirit. Evils of the heart, of the mind, of the
soul, of the spirit—these have to do with man's
sin, and the only reason the human body does evil
is because the human spirit uses it to do evil.
*A. W. Tozer*

Abhor that which is evil;
cleave to that which is good.
*Romans 12:9 KJV*

Dear Lord, because You have given Your children
free will, the world is a place where evil
threatens our lives and our souls. Protect us,
Father, from the evils and temptations of this
difficult age. Help us to trust You, Father, and to
obey Your Word, knowing that Your ultimate
victory over evil is inevitable and complete.
—Amen—

# FAITH

Let us run with endurance the race that
is set before us, fixing our eyes on Jesus,
the author and perfecter of faith.

*Hebrews 12:1-2 NASB*

Have you ever felt your faith in God slipping away? If so, you are not alone. Every life—including yours—is a series of successes and failures, celebrations and disappointments, joys and sorrows. But even when we feel very distant from God, God is never distant from us.

Jesus taught His disciples that if they had faith, they could move mountains. You can too. When you place your faith, your trust, indeed your life, in the hands of Christ Jesus, you'll be amazed at the marvelous things He can do with you and through you. So strengthen your faith through praise, through worship, through Bible study, and through prayer. And trust God's plans. With Him, all things are possible, and He stands ready to open a world of possibilities to you if you have faith.

The measure of faith must always determine the
measure of power and of blessing. Faith can only
live by feeding on what is Divine, on God Himself.

*Andrew Murray*

# THE POWER OF FAITH

Little faith will bring your soul to heaven;
great faith will bring heaven to your soul.
*C. H. Spurgeon*

Faith sees the invisible, believes the unbelievable,
and receives the impossible.
*Corrie ten Boom*

I tell you the truth, if you have faith as small
as a mustard seed, you can say to this mountain,
"Move from here to there" and it will move.
Nothing will be impossible for you.
*Matthew 17:20 NIV*

Father, in the dark moments of my life, help me
to remember that You are always near and that
You can overcome any challenge. Keep me
mindful of Your love and Your power, so that
I may live courageously and faithfully
today and every day.
—Amen—

# FAMILY

But if anyone does not provide for his own, and
especially for those of his household, he has denied
the faith and is worse than an unbeliever.

*1 Timothy 5:8 NASB*

The words of 2 Timothy 5:8 are unambiguous: if God has blessed us with families, then He expects us to care for them. Sometimes, this profound responsibility seems daunting. And sometimes, even for the most dedicated Christian men, family life holds moments of frustration and disappointment. But, for those who are lucky enough to live in the presence of a close-knit, caring clan, the rewards far outweigh the demands.

No family is perfect, and neither is yours. Despite the inevitable challenges of providing for your family, and despite the occasional hurt feelings of family life, your clan is God's gift to you. Give thanks to the Giver for the gift of family . . . and act accordingly.

Never give your family the leftovers
and crumbs of your time.

*Charles Swindoll*

# A Forgiving Heart

Forgiveness is God's command.

*Martin Luther*

Miracles broke the physical laws of the universe;
forgiveness broke the moral rules.

*Philip Yancey*

Judge not, and ye shall not be judged:
condemn not, and ye shall not be condemned:
forgive, and ye shall be forgiven.

*Luke 6:37 KJV*

Heavenly Father, sometimes I am tempted
to strike out at those who have hurt me. Keep me
mindful that forgiveness is Your commandment.
You have forgiven me, Lord; let me show my
thankfulness to You by offering forgiveness to
others. And, when I do, may others see Your love
reflected through my words and deeds.

—Amen—

# FRIENDSHIP

A friend loves at all times,
and a brother is born for adversity.
*Proverbs 17:17 NIV*

Friend: a one-syllable word describing "a person who is attached to another by feelings of affection or personal regard." This definition, or one very similar to it, can be found in any dictionary, but genuine friendship is much more. When we consider the deeper meaning of friendship, so many descriptors come to mind: trustworthiness, loyalty, helpfulness, kindness, understanding, forgiveness, encouragement, humor, and cheerfulness, to mention but a few.

The familiar words of 1 Corinthians 13:2 remind us that love and charity are among God's greatest gifts: "And though I have the gift of prophecy, and understand all mysteries, and all knowledge; and though I have all faith, so that I could remove mountains, and have not charity, I am nothing" (KJV). Today and every day, resolve to be a trustworthy, encouraging, loyal friend. And, treasure the people in your life who are loyal friends to you. Friendship is, after all, a glorious gift, praised by God. Give thanks for that gift and nurture it.

# The Joy of Friendship

You could have been born in another time and
another place, but God determined to "people"
your life with these particular friends.

*Joni Eareckson Tada*

Friendship is one of the sweetest joys of life.
Many might have failed beneath the bitterness of
their trial had they not found a friend.

*C. H. Spurgeon*

I give thanks to my God
for every remembrance of you.

*Philippians 1:3 HCSB*

Lord, thank You for my friends. Let me be
a trustworthy friend to others, and let my love for
You be reflected in my genuine love for them.

—Amen—

# GENEROSITY

Now this I say, he who sows sparingly will also reap sparingly, and he who sows bountifully will also reap bountifully. Each one must do just as he has purposed in his heart, not grudgingly or under compulsion, for God loves a cheerful giver.

*2 Corinthians 9:6-7 NASB*

The words of Jesus are clear: "Freely you have received, freely give" (Matthew 10:8 NIV). As followers of Christ, we are commanded to be generous with our friends, with our families, and with those in need. We must give freely of our time, our possessions, and, most especially, our love. Paul reminds us, in 2 Corinthians 9, that when we sow the seeds of generosity, we reap bountiful rewards in accordance with God's plan for our lives. But Paul offers a word of caution: We are commanded to be cheerful givers—not to give "grudgingly or under compulsion."

Today, take God's words to heart and make this pledge: be a cheerful, generous, courageous giver. The world needs your help, and you need the spiritual rewards that will be yours when you do.

# THE JOY OF GIVING

I can usually sense that a leading is from the Holy
Spirit when it calls me to humble myself, to serve
somebody, to encourage somebody, or to give
something away. Very rarely will the evil one lead
us to do those kinds of things.

*Bill Hybels*


The mind grows by taking in, but the heart grows
by giving out.

*Warren Wiersbe*


I tell you the truth, whatever you did for one of
the least of these brothers of mine, you did for me.

*Matthew 25:40 NIV*

Lord, You have been so generous with me;
let me be generous with others. Help me to give
generously of my time and my possessions as
I care for those in need. And, make me a humble
giver, Lord, so that all the glory and
the praise might be Yours.

—Amen—

# GIFTS

Every good gift and every perfect gift is from
above, and cometh down from the Father of lights.

*James 1:17 KJV*

All men possess special gifts—bestowed from
the Father above—and you are no
exception. But, your gift is no guarantee of success;
it must be cultivated and nurtured; otherwise, it will
go unused...and God's gift to you will be squandered.

Today, make a promise to yourself that you will
earnestly seek to discover the talents that God has
given you. Then, nourish those talents and make
them grow. Finally, vow to share your gifts with the
world for as long as God gives you the power to do
so. After all, the best way to say "Thank You" for
God's gifts is to use them.

God is still in the process of dispensing gifts, and
He uses ordinary individuals like us to develop
those gifts in other people.

*Howard Hendricks*

# THOUGHTS ON GOD'S GIFTS

When God crowns our merits,
He is crowning nothing other than his gifts.

*St. Augustine*

The Lord has abundantly blessed me all of my life.
I'm not trying to pay Him back for all of
His wonderful gifts; I just realize that He gave
them to me to give away.

*Lisa Whelchel*

Each man has his own gift from God;
one has this gift, another has that.

*1 Corinthians 7:7 NIV*

Lord, I praise You for Your priceless gifts. I give
thanks for Your creation, for Your Son, and
for the unique talents and opportunities that You
have given me. Let me use my gifts for
the glory of Your kingdom, this day and every day.

—Amen—

# GOD'S COMMANDMENTS

My son, do not forget my teaching,
but let your heart keep my commandments.

*Proverbs 3:1 NASB*

A life of righteousness is lived in accordance with God's commandments. A righteous man strives to be faithful, honest, generous, disciplined, loving, kind, humble, and grateful, to name only a few of the more obvious qualities which are described in God's Word.

If we seek to follow the steps of Jesus, we must seek to live according to His teachings. In short, we must, to the best of our abilities, live according to the principles contained in the Holy Bible. When we do, we become powerful examples to our families and friends of the blessings that God bestows upon righteous men.

Bible history is filled with people who began
the race with great success but failed at the end
because they disregarded God's rules.

*Warren Wiersbe*

# Thoughts on God's Laws

God's word is not obsolete; it is absolute.
*Vance Havner*

Faith reposes on the character of God, and
if we believe that God is perfect, we must conclude
that his ways are perfect also.
*A. W. Tozer*

This is how we are sure that we have come to
know Him: by keeping His commands.
*1 John 2:3 HCSB*

Father, Your commandments are perfect and
everlasting; let me use them as a guide for my life.
Let me obey Your Word, and let me lead others
to do the same. Make me a man of wisdom,
and let me walk righteously in Your way,
Dear Lord, trusting always in You.
—Amen—

# GOD'S LOVE

The unfailing love of the LORD never ends!
*Lamentations 3:22 NLT*

God loves you. Period. He loves you more than you can imagine; His affection is deeper and more profound than you can fathom. God made you in His own image and gave you salvation through the person of His Son Jesus Christ. And now, precisely because you are a wondrous creation treasured by God, a question presents itself: what will you do in response to God's love? Will you ignore it or embrace it? Will you return it or neglect it? The decision, of course, is yours and yours alone.

When you embrace God's love, you are forever changed. When you embrace God's love, you feel differently about yourself, your neighbors, and your world. More importantly, you share God's message— and His love—with others.

God offers His love freely. Accept it. Today. Period.

The great love of God is an ocean
without a bottom or a shore.
*C. H. Spurgeon*

# GOD'S EVERLASTING LOVE

If you have a true faith that Christ is your Savior,
then at once you have a gracious God,
for faith leads you in and opens up God's heart
and will, that you should see pure grace
and overflowing love.

*Martin Luther*


The greatest love of all is God's love for us,
a love that showed itself in action.

*Billy Graham*


But the love of the LORD remains forever with
those who fear him. His salvation extends to the
children's children of those who are faithful to his
covenant, of those who obey his commandments!

*Psalm 103:17-18 NLT*


God, You are love. I love You, Lord, and
as I love You more, I am able to love my family
and friends more. Let me be Your loving servant,
Heavenly Father, today and throughout eternity.

—Amen—

# GOD'S MERCY

But because of his great love for us, God,
who is rich in mercy, made us alive with Christ
even when we were dead in transgressions—
it is by grace you have been saved.

*Ephesians 2:4-5 NIV*

God's ability to forgive is as infinite as His love. Romans 3:23 reminds us of a universal truth: "All have sinned, and come short of the glory of God" (KJV). All of us, even the most righteous among us, are sinners. But despite our imperfections, our Father in heaven offers us salvation through the person of His Son.

God sent Jesus to die so that we might have eternal life. As Christians, we have been blessed by a merciful, loving God. May we accept His mercy. And may we, in turn, show love and mercy to our friends, to our families, and to all whom He chooses to place in our paths.

God's mercy is infinite, but it always flows
to men through the golden channel
of Jesus Christ, his son.

*C. H. Spurgeon*

# THOUGHTS ON GOD'S
# EVERLASTING MERCY

God's heart of mercy provides for us not only
pardon from sin but also a daily provision
of spiritual food to strengthen us.

*Jim Cymbala*

God is more anxious to bestow His blessings
on us than we are to receive them.

*St. Augustine*

The LORD is gracious and compassionate,
slow to anger and rich in love. The LORD is good
to all; he has compassion on all he has made.

*Psalm 145:8-9 NIV*

Dear Lord, I have fallen short of Your
commandments, and You have forgiven me.
You have blessed me with Your love and Your
mercy. Enable me to be merciful toward others,
Father, just as You have been merciful to me, and
let me share Your love with all whom I meet.

—Amen—

# GOD'S PLAN

The LORD will work out his plans for my life—
for your faithful love, O LORD, endures forever.

*Psalm 138:8 NLT*

God has plans for your life, but He won't force those plans upon you. To the contrary, He has given you free will, the ability to make decisions on your own. With that freedom to choose comes the responsibility of living with the consequences of the choices you make.

If you seek to live in accordance with God's will for your life—and you should—then you will live in accordance with His commandments. You will study God's Word, and you will be watchful for His signs. You will associate with fellow Christians who will encourage your spiritual growth, and you will listen to that inner voice that speaks to you in the quiet moments of your daily devotionals. God intends to use you in wonderful, unexpected ways if you let Him. The decision to seek God's plan and to follow it is yours and yours alone. The consequences of that decision have implications that are both profound and eternal, so choose carefully.

Faith never knows where it is being led,
but it loves the One who is leading.

*Oswald Chambers*

# Thoughts on God's Plan

If not a sparrow falls upon the ground without your
Father, you have reason to see that the smallest
events of your career are arranged by him.

*C. H. Spurgeon*

Seeing that a Pilot steers the ship in which we sail,
who will never allow us to perish even in the
midst of shipwrecks, there is no reason why our
minds should be overwhelmed with fear and
overcome with weariness.

*John Calvin*

It is God who works in you to will and
to act according to his good purpose.

*Philippians 2:13 NIV*

Lord, today, I will seek Your will for my life.
You have a plan for me, Father. Let me discover it
and live it, knowing that when I trust in You
I am eternally blessed.

—Amen—

# GOD'S PROMISES

Heaven and earth will pass away,
but my words will never pass away.

*Matthew 24:35 NIV*

The Bible contains promises, made by God, upon which we, as believers, can and must depend. But sometimes, especially when we find ourselves caught in the inevitable entanglements of life, we fail to trust God completely.

Are you tired? Discouraged? Fearful? Be comforted and trust the promises that God has made to you. Are you worried or anxious? Be confident in God's power. Do you see a difficult future ahead? Be courageous and call upon God. He will protect you and then use you according to His purposes. Are you confused? Listen to the quiet voice of your Heavenly Father. He is not a God of confusion. Talk with Him; listen to Him; trust Him, and trust His promises. He is steadfast, and He is your Protector...forever.

God's promises are overflowings
from his great heart.

*C. H. Spurgeon*

# Trusting God's Promises

Only God knows when everything in and
around is fully ripe for the manifestation of
the blessings that have been given to faith
(Mark 11:24). It is through faith and
patience we inherit the promises.

*Andrew Murray*


Whosoever cometh to me, and heareth
my sayings, and doeth them, I will show you to
whom he is like: he is like a man which built
a house, and digged deep, and laid the foundation
on a rock: and when the flood arose, the stream
beat vehemently upon that house, and could not
shake it; for it was founded upon a rock.

*Luke 6:47-48 KJV*


Lord, Your Holy Word contains promises, and
I will trust them. I will use the Bible as my guide,
and I will trust You, Lord, to speak to me through
Your Holy Spirit and through Your Holy Word,
this day and forever.

—Amen—

# GOD'S PROTECTION

I know the LORD is always with me.
I will not be shaken, for he is right beside me.
*Psalm 16:8 NLT*

God loves us and protects us. In times of trouble, He comforts us; in times of sorrow, He dries our tears. Psalm 147 promises, "He heals the brokenhearted, and binds their wounds" (v. 3 NASB). When we are troubled, we must call upon God, and—in His own time and according to His own plan—He will heal us.

Do you feel fearful or weak or sorrowful? Are you discouraged or bitter? Do you feel "stuck" in a place that is uncomfortable for you? If so, remember that God is as near as your next breath. So trust Him and turn to Him for solace, for security, and for salvation. And build your life on the rock that cannot be shaken . . . that rock is God.

As sure as God puts his children in the furnace,
He will be in the furnace with them.
*C. H. Spurgeon*

# Thoughts on God's Protection

The Rock of Ages is the great
sheltering encirclement.

*Oswald Chambers*

When you are in the furnace, your Father keeps
His eye on the clock and His hand on
the thermostat. He knows just how
much we can take.

*Warren Wiersbe*

Seek the LORD, and his strength: seek his face
evermore. Remember his marvelous works.

*Psalm 105:4-5 KJV*

Lord, You have promised that You will provide for
my needs, and I trust that promise. But sometimes,
because of my imperfect faith, I fall prey to worry
and doubt. Today, give me the courage to trust You
completely. You are my Protector, Dear Lord;
let me praise You, let me love You, and let me
trust in the perfect wisdom of Your plan.

—Amen—

# GOD'S WORD

But He answered, "It is written: Man must
not live on bread alone, but on every word that
comes from the mouth of God."

*Matthew 4:4 HCSB*

The Bible is unlike any other book. It is a
priceless gift from our Creator, a tool that
God intends for us to use in every aspect of our lives.
And, it contains promises upon which we, as
Christians, can and must depend.

Are you tired? Discouraged? Concerned about
an uncertain future? Then open your Bible and read
it with a focused mind and an open heart. You can
trust the promises that you find there.

Are you worried or anxious? Be confident in
God's power. He will never desert you. Do you see a
difficult future ahead? Be courageous and call upon
God. He will protect you and then use you according
to His purposes. Are you confused? Listen to the quiet
voice of your Heavenly Father. He is not a God of
confusion. Talk with Him; listen to Him; trust Him,
and trust His promises. He is steadfast, and He is
your Protector . . . forever.

It takes calm, thoughtful, prayerful meditation on
the Word to extract its deepest nourishment.

*Vance Havner*

# THOUGHTS ON THE POWER
## OF GOD'S WORD

The promises of Scripture are not mere pious
hopes or sanctified guesses. They are more
than sentimental words to be printed on
decorated cards for Sunday School children.
They are eternal verities. They are true.
There is no perhaps about them.

*Peter Marshall*


The vigor of our spiritual lives will be in exact
proportion to the place held by the Bible
in our lives and in our thoughts.

*George Mueller*


Thy word is a lamp unto my feet,
and a light unto my path.

*Psalm 119:105 KJV*

Dear Lord, the Bible is Your gift to me; let me
use it. When I stray from Your Holy Word, Lord,
I suffer. But, when I place Your Word at the very
center of my life, I am blessed. Make me a faithful
student of Your Word so that I might be a faithful
servant in Your world, this day and every day.

—Amen—

# THE GOLDEN RULE

So in everything, do to others what you
would have them do to you, for this sums up
the Law and the Prophets.

*Matthew 7:12 NIV*

How should we treat other people? God's Word is clear: we should treat others in the same way that we wish to be treated. This Golden Rule is easy to understand, but sometimes it can be difficult to live by.

Because we are imperfect human beings, we are, on occasion, selfish, thoughtless, or cruel. But God commands us to behave otherwise. He teaches us to rise above our own imperfections and to treat others with unselfishness and love. When we observe God's Golden Rule, we help build His kingdom here on earth. And, when we share the love of Christ, we share a priceless gift; may we share it today and every day that we live.

He climbs highest who helps another up.

*Zig Ziglar*

# Applying the Golden Rule

All kindness and good deeds, we must keep silent.
The result will be an inner reservoir
of personality power.
*Catherine Marshall*


Good will is written into the constitution
of things; ill will is sand in the machinery.

*E. Stanley Jones*


Bear ye one another's burdens,
and so fulfill the law of Christ.
*Galatians 6:2 KJV*


Dear Lord, let me treat others as I wish to be
treated. Because I expect kindness, let me be kind.
Because I wish to be loved, let me be loving.
Because I need forgiveness, let me be merciful.
In all things, Lord, let me live by the Golden Rule,
and let me teach that rule to others through
my words and my deeds.
—Amen—

# GRACE

For by grace are ye saved through faith;
and that not of yourselves: it is the gift of God:
not of works, lest any man should boast.

*Ephesians 2:8-9 KJV*

We have received countless gifts from God, but none can compare with the gift of salvation. When we accept Christ into our hearts, we are saved by God's grace. The familiar words of Ephesians 2:8 make God's promise perfectly clear: we are saved not by our actions, but by God's mercy. We are saved not because of our good deeds, but because of our faith in Christ.

God's grace is the ultimate gift, and we owe Him the ultimate in thanksgiving. Let us praise the Creator for His priceless gift, and let us share the good news with all who cross our paths. We return our Father's love by accepting His grace and by sharing His message and His love. When we do, we are blessed here on earth and throughout all eternity.

We shall grow in grace, but we shall never be
more completely pardoned than
the moment we first believed.

*C. H. Spurgeon*

# THE GIFT OF GOD'S GRACE

The grace of God is sufficient for all our needs,
for every problem, and for every difficulty, for every
broken heart, and for every human sorrow.

*Peter Marshall*

Faith is a living, daring confidence in God's grace,
so sure and certain that a man would stake
his life on it a thousand times.

*Martin Luther*

Therefore let us draw near with confidence to
the throne of grace, so that we may receive mercy
and find grace to help in time of need.

*Hebrews 4:16 NASB*

Lord, You have saved me by Your grace.
Keep me mindful that Your grace is a gift that
I can accept but cannot earn. I praise You for that
priceless gift, today and forever. Let me share
the good news of Your grace with a world that
desperately needs Your healing touch.

—Amen—

# GRIEF

The LORD shall give thee rest from thy sorrow,
and from thy fear.

*Isaiah 14:3 KJV*

Grief visits all of us who live long and love deeply. When we lose a loved one, or when we experience any other profound loss, darkness overwhelms us for a while, and it seems as if we cannot summon the strength to face another day—but, with God's help, we can. When our friends or family members encounter life-shattering events, we struggle to find words that might offer them comfort and support. But finding the right words can be difficult, if not impossible. Sometimes, all that we can do is to be with our loved ones, offering them few words but much love.

Thankfully, God promises that He is "close to the brokenhearted" (Psalm 34:18 NIV). In times of intense sadness, we must turn to Him, and we must encourage our friends and family members to do likewise. When we do, our Father comforts us and, in time, He heals us.

Tears are permitted to us, but they must glisten
in the light of faith and hope.

*C. H. Spurgeon*

# Accepting God's Comfort

In heaven, we will see that nothing, absolutely
nothing, was wasted, and that every tear counted
and every cry was heard.

*Joni Eareckson Tada*

When I am criticized, injured, or afraid,
there is a Father who is ready to comfort me.

*Max Lucado*

Ye shall be sorrowful, but your sorrow
shall be turned into joy.

*John 16:20 KJV*

Heavenly Father, Your Word promises that
You will not give us more than we can bear;
You have promised to lift us out of our grief and
despair. Today, Lord, I pray for those who mourn,
and I thank You for sustaining all of us in our
days of sorrow. May we trust You always
and praise You forever.

—Amen—

# HOPE

May the God of hope fill you with all joy and
peace as you trust in him, so that you may overflow
with hope by the power of the Holy Spirit.

*Romans 15:13 NIV*

Despite God's promises, despite Christ's love, and despite our countless blessings, we frail human beings can still lose hope from time to time. When we do, we need the encouragement of Christian friends, the life-changing power of prayer, and the healing truth of God's Holy Word.

If you find yourself falling into the spiritual traps of worry and discouragement, seek the healing touch of Jesus and the encouraging words of fellow Christians. And remember the words of our Savior: "These things I have spoken unto you, that in me ye might have peace. In the world ye shall have tribulation: but be of good cheer; I have overcome the world" (John 16:33 KJV). This world can be a place of trials and tribulations, but as believers, we are secure. God has promised us peace, joy, and eternal life. And, of course, God keeps His promises today, tomorrow, and forever.

Everything that is done in
the world is done by hope.

*Martin Luther*

# THE POWER OF HOPE

Oh, remember this: There is never a time
when we may not hope in God. Whatever our
necessities, however great our difficulties, and
though to all appearance, help is impossible, yet
our business is to hope in God, and it will be
found that it is not in vain.

*George Mueller*


Hope is no other than the expectation of those
things which faith has believed to be truly
promised by God.

*John Calvin*


For we are saved by hope....

*Romans 8:24 KJV*

***


Today, Dear Lord, I will live in hope. If I become
discouraged, I will turn to You. If I grow weary,
I will seek strength in You. In every aspect of my
life, I will trust You. You are my Father, Lord,
and I place my hope and my faith in You.

—Amen—

# INTEGRITY

The just man walketh in his integrity:
his children are blessed after him.

*Proverbs 20:7 KJV*

It has been said on many occasions and in many ways that honesty is the best policy. For believers, it is far more important to note that honesty is God's policy. And if we are to be servants worthy of our Savior, Jesus Christ, we must be honest and forthright in our communications with others. Sometimes, honesty is difficult; sometimes, honesty is painful; sometimes, honesty is inconvenient; but always honesty is God's commandment.

In the Book of Proverbs, we read, "The LORD detests lying lips, but he delights in men who are truthful" (12:22 NIV). Clearly, truth is God's way, and it must be our way, too, even when telling the truth is difficult.

Image is what people think we are;
integrity is what we really are.

*John Maxwell*

# A Life of Integrity

Integrity is the glue that holds our way of life together. We must constantly strive to keep our integrity intact. When wealth is lost, nothing is lost; when health is lost, something is lost; when character is lost, all is lost.

*Billy Graham*

Maintaining your integrity in a world of sham is no small accomplishment.

*Wayne Oates*

Lead a tranquil and quiet life in all godliness and dignity.

*1 Timothy 2:2 HCSB*

Dear Lord, You command Your children to walk in truth. Let me follow Your commandment. Give me the courage to speak honestly, and let me walk righteously with You so that others might see Your eternal truth reflected in my words and my deeds.

—Amen—

# JOY

Shout for joy to the LORD, all the earth.
Worship the LORD with gladness;
come before him with joyful songs.

*Psalm 100:1-2 NIV*

The Bible makes it clear: God intends that His joy should become our joy. As believers who have been saved by a loving and merciful God, we have every reason to celebrate. Yet sometimes, amid the inevitable hustle and bustle of life here on earth, we can forfeit—albeit temporarily—the joy that God has in store for us.

This day is a gift from the Creator. Let us celebrate it cheerfully; let us worship Him with thanks in our hearts and praise on our lips. Let us raise our thoughts and our prayers to Him. And let us accept the joy that is the spiritual birthright of those who have been touched and saved by the Master's hand.

Joy comes not from what we have
but from what we are.

*C. H. Spurgeon*

# JOY TO THE WORLD!

God knows everything. He can manage
everything, and He loves us. Surely this is enough
for a fullness of joy that is beyond words.

*Hannah Whitall Smith*

God can take any man and put the miracle
of His joy into him.

*Oswald Chambers*

Rejoice, and be exceeding glad:
for great is your reward in heaven....

*Matthew 5:12 KJV*

+≈≈+

Lord, make me a joyous Christian. Because of
my salvation through Your Son, I have every
reason to celebrate life. Let me share the joyful
news of Jesus Christ, and let my life be
a testimony to His love and to His grace.

—Amen—

# KINDNESS

So, as those who have been chosen of God,
holy and beloved, put on a heart of compassion,
kindness, humility, gentleness and patience.

*Colossians 3:12 NASB*

The instructions of Colossians 3:12 are unambiguous: as Christians, we are to be compassionate, humble, gentle, and kind. But sometimes, of course, we fall short. In the busyness and confusion of daily life, we may neglect to share a kind word or a kind deed. This oversight hurts others, but it hurts us most of all.

Today, slow yourself down and be alert for those who need your smile, your kind words, or your helping hand. Make kindness a centerpiece of your dealings with others. They will be blessed, and you will be too. Today, honor Christ by following His Golden Rule. He expects no less, and He deserves no less.

It's not difficult to make an impact on your world.
All you really have to do is put the needs of others
ahead of your own. You can make a difference
with a little time and a big heart.

*James Dobson*

# THOUGHTS ON KINDNESS

When you extend hospitality to others,
you're not trying to impress people,
you're trying to reflect God to them.
*Max Lucado*

People don't care how much you know until
they know how much you care.
*John Maxwell*

. . . be gentle to everyone, able to teach,
and patient.
*2 Timothy 2:24 HCSB*

Lord, make me a loving, encouraging Christian.
And, let my love for Christ be reflected through
the kindness that I show to those who need
the healing touch of the Master's hand.
—Amen—

# LAUGHTER

A cheerful heart is good medicine.

*Proverbs 17:22 NIV*

Laughter is God's gift, and He intends that we enjoy it. Yet sometimes, because of the inevitable stresses of everyday life, laughter seems only a distant memory. As Christians we have every reason to be cheerful and to be thankful. Our blessings from God are beyond measure, starting, of course, with a gift that is ours for the asking: God's gift of salvation through Christ Jesus.

Few things in life are more absurd than the sight of a grumpy Christian. So today, as you go about your daily activities, approach life with a smile and a chuckle. After all, God created laughter for a reason…and Father indeed knows best. So laugh!

It is often just as sacred to laugh as it is to pray.

*Charles Swindoll*

# THE IMPORTANCE OF LAUGHTER

Laughter dulls the sharpest pain and
flattens out the greatest stress. To share it is
to give a gift of health.

*Barbara Johnson*


If you're not allowed to laugh in heaven,
don't want to go there.

*Martin Luther*


Humor ought to be consecrated and
used for the cause of Christ.

*C. H. Spurgeon*


A joyful heart makes a cheerful face.

*Proverbs 15:13 NASB*


Dear Lord, laughter is Your gift.
Today and every day, put a smile on my face,
and let me share that smile with all who cross
my path…and let me laugh.

—Amen—

# LEADERSHIP

We have different gifts, according to the grace
given us. If a man's gift is prophesying, let him
use it in proportion to his faith. If it is serving,
let him serve; if it is teaching, let him teach;
if it is encouraging, let him encourage; . . .
if it is leadership, let him govern diligently;
if it is showing mercy, let him do it cheerfully.

*Romans 12:6-8 NIV*

John Maxwell writes, "Great leaders understand that the right attitude will set the right
atmosphere, which enables the right response from
others." If you are in a position of leadership whether
as a father—or as a leader at your work, your church,
or your school—it's up to you to set the right tone by
maintaining the right attitude. What's your attitude
today? Are you fearful, angry, bored, or worried? Are
you confused, bitter, or pessimistic? If so, then you
should ask yourself if you're the kind of leader whom
you would want to follow. If the answer to that
question is no, then it's time to improve your
leadership skills.

Our world needs Christian leadership, and so do
your family members and coworkers. You can become
a trusted, competent, thoughtful leader if you learn
to maintain the right attitude: one that is realistic,
optimistic, forward looking, and Christ-centered.

# THOUGHTS ON LEADERSHIP

Leaders must learn how to wait.
Often their followers don't always see as far
as they see or have the faith that they have.
*Warren Wiersbe*


You can never separate a leader's actions
from his character.
*John Maxwell*


Those who are wise will shine like the brightness
of the heavens, and those who lead many to
righteousness, like the stars for ever and ever.
*Daniel 12:3 NIV*


Heavenly Father, when I find myself in
a position of leadership, let me follow
Your teachings and obey Your commandments.
Make me a man of integrity and wisdom, Lord,
and make me a worthy example to those whom
I serve. Let me turn to You, Lord, for guidance and
for strength in all that I say and do.
—Amen—

# LOVE

But now abide faith, hope, love, these three;
but the greatest of these is love.

*1 Corinthians 13:13 NASB*

The familiar words of 1 Corinthians 13 remind us that love is God's commandment. Faith is important, of course. So too is hope. But love is more important still.

Christ showed His love for us on the cross, and, as Christians, we are called upon to return Christ's love by sharing it. We are commanded (not advised, not encouraged . . . commanded!) to love one another just as Christ loved us (John 13:34). That's a tall order, but as Christians, we are obligated to follow it.

Sometimes love is easy (puppies and sleeping children come to mind) and sometimes love is hard (fallible human beings come to mind). But God's Word is clear: we are to love all of our neighbors, not just the lovable ones. So today, take time to spread Christ's message by word and by example. And the greatest of these is example.

The world does not understand theology or dogma, but it does understand love and sympathy.

*D. L. Moody*

# THE POWER OF LOVE

Carve your name on hearts, not on marble.
*C. H. Spurgeon*

Beware that you are not swallowed up in books!
An ounce of love is worth a pound of knowledge.
*John Wesley*

He who is filled with love is filled
with God Himself.
*St. Augustine*

Let love and faithfulness never leave you…
write them on the tablet of your heart.
*Proverbs 3:3 NIV*

Dear Lord, You have given me the gift of love;
let me share that gift with others. And, keep me
mindful that the essence of love is not
to receive it, but to give it, today and forever.
—Amen—

# MIRACLES

But Jesus beheld them, and said unto them,
"With men this is impossible;
but with God all things are possible."
*Matthew 19:26 KJV*

Sometimes, because we are imperfect human beings with limited understanding and limited faith, we place limitations on God. But, God's power has no limitations. God will work miracles in our lives if we trust Him with everything we have and everything we are. When we do, we experience the miraculous results of His endless love and His awesome power.

Do you lack the faith that God can work miracles in your own life? If so, it's time to reconsider. Are you a "Doubting Thomas" or a "Negative Ned"? If so, you are attempting to place limitations on a God who has none. Instead, you must trust in God and trust in His power. Then, you must wait patiently, because something miraculous is about to happen.

We have a God who delights in impossibilities.
*Andrew Murray*

# FORGIVENESS

Be kind to one another, tender-hearted,
forgiving each other, just as God in Christ
also has forgiven you.

*Ephesians 4:32 NASB*

It has been said that life is an exercise in forgiveness. How true. Christ understood the importance of forgiveness when he commanded, "Love your enemies and pray for those who persecute you" (Matthew 5:43-44 NIV). But sometimes, forgiveness is difficult indeed. When we have been injured or embarrassed, we feel the urge to strike back and to hurt the one who has hurt us. Christ instructs us to do otherwise. Believers are taught that forgiveness is God's way and that mercy is an integral part of God's plan for our lives.

If there exists even one person, alive or dead, whom you have not forgiven (including yourself), follow God's commandment and His will for your life: forgive. Hatred and bitterness and regret are not part of God's plan for your life. Forgiveness is.

To be a Christian means to forgive
the inexcusable, because God has forgiven
the inexcusable in you.

*C. S. Lewis*

# THE JOYS OF FAMILY LIFE

No other structure can replace the family.
Without it, our children have no moral
foundation. Without it, they become moral
illiterates whose only law is self.
*Chuck Colson*

There is always room for more loving
forgiveness within our homes.
*James Dobson*

Choose for yourselves this day whom
you will serve…as for me and my household,
we will serve the LORD.
*Joshua 24:15 NIV*

Dear Lord, I am blessed to be part of the family
of God where I find love and acceptance. You
have also blessed me with my earthly family.
Let me show love and acceptance for my own
family so that through me they might
come to know You.
—Amen—

# TRUSTING GOD'S POWER

Only God can move mountains, but faith
and prayer can move God.
*E. M. Bounds*

There is Someone who makes possible
what seems completely impossible.
*Catherine Marshall*

Now we have received, not the spirit of the world,
but the Spirit which is of God; that we might
know the things that are freely given to us of God.
*1 Corinthians 2:12 KJV*

Dear God, nothing is impossible for You. Your
infinite power is beyond human understanding—
keep me always mindful of Your strength. When
I lose hope, give me faith; when others lose hope,
let me tell them of Your glory and Your works.
Today, Lord, let me expect the miraculous,
and let me trust in You.
—Amen—

# OBEDIENCE

Blessed are they who maintain justice,
who constantly do what is right.

*Psalm 106:3 NIV*

Since God created Adam and Eve, we human beings have been rebelling against our Creator. Why? Because we are unwilling to trust God's Word, and we are unwilling to follow His commandments. God has given us a guidebook for righteous living called the Holy Bible. It contains thorough instructions which, if followed, lead to fulfillment, righteousness, and salvation. But, if we choose to ignore God's commandments, the results are as predictable as they are tragic.

Talking about God is easy; living by His commandments is considerably harder. But, unless we are willing to abide by God's laws, all of our righteous proclamations ring hollow. How can we best proclaim our love for the Lord? By obeying Him. And, for further instructions, read the manual.

Faith is obedience at home and looking to
the Master; obedience is faith
going out to do His will.

*Andrew Murray*

# OBEYING GOD'S LAWS

Obedience that is not motivated by love
cannot produce the spiritual fruit that God
wants from His children.

*Warren Wiersbe*

And, behold, one came and said unto him,
Good Master, what good thing shall I do,
that I may have eternal life? And he said unto
him, Why callest thou me good? there is none
good but one, that is, God: but if thou wilt enter
into life, keep the commandments.

*Matthew 19:16-17 KJV*

Heavenly Father, when I turn my thoughts
away from You and Your Word, I suffer. But when
I obey Your commandments, when I place my faith
in You, I am secure. Let me live according to Your
commandments. Direct my path far from
the temptations and distractions of this world.
And, let me discover Your will and follow it,
Dear Lord, this day and always.
—Amen—

# OPTIMISM

The LORD is my light and my salvation;
whom shall I fear? The LORD is the strength
of my life; of whom shall I be afraid?

*Psalm 27:1 KJV*

Christians have every reason to be optimistic about life. As John Calvin observed, "There is not one blade of grass, there is no color in this world that is not intended to make us rejoice." But, sometimes, rejoicing is the last thing on our minds. Sometimes, we fall prey to worry, frustration, anxiety, or sheer exhaustion, and our hearts become heavy. What's needed is plenty of rest, a large dose of perspective, and God's healing touch, but not necessarily in that order.

Today, why not claim the joy that is rightfully yours in Christ? Why not take time to celebrate God's glorious creation? Why not trust your hopes instead of your fears? When you do, you will think optimistically about yourself and your world…and you can then share your optimism with others. They'll be better for it, and so will you. But not necessarily in that order.

If our hearts have been attuned to God through
an abiding faith in Christ, the result will be
joyous optimism and good cheer.

*Billy Graham*

# THE POWER OF OPTIMISM AND FAITH

Keep your feet on the ground, but let your
heart soar as high as it will. Refuse to be average
or to surrender to the chill of your
spiritual environment.

*A. W. Tozer*

The essence of optimism is that it takes no
account of the present, but it is a source of
inspiration, of vitality, and of hope. Where others
have resigned, it enables a man to hold his head
high, to claim the future for himself, and
not abandon it to his enemy.

*Dietrich Bonhoeffer*

The fundamental fact of existence is that this trust
in God, this faith, is the firm foundation under
everything that makes life worth living.

*Hebrews 11:1 MSG*

Lord, give me faith, optimism, and hope.
Let me expect the best from You, and let me look
for the best in others. Let me trust You, Lord,
to direct my life. And, let me be Your faithful,
hopeful, optimistic servant every day that I live.

—Amen—

# PATIENCE

Better a patient man than a warrior, a man who
controls his temper than one who takes a city.
*Proverbs 16:32 NIV*

L ife demands patience . . . and lots of it! We
live in an imperfect world inhabited by
imperfect people. Sometimes, we inherit troubles
from others, and sometimes we create trouble for
ourselves. In either case, what's required is patience.
Lamentations 3:25-26 reminds us that, "The LORD
is wonderfully good to those who wait for him and
seek him. So it is good to wait quietly for salvation
from the LORD" (NLT). But, for most of us, waiting
quietly for God is difficult. Why? Because we are
fallible human beings, sometimes quick to anger and
sometimes slow to forgive.

The next time you find your patience tested to
the limit, remember that the world unfolds according
to God's timetable, not ours. Sometimes, we must
wait patiently, and that's as it should be. After all,
think how patient God has been with us.

By his wisdom, he orders his delays so that they
prove to be far better than our hurries.
C. H. *Spurgeon*

# THE POWER OF PATIENCE

Patience is the companion of wisdom.

*St. Augustine*

The challenge before us is to have faith in God,
and the hardest part of faith is waiting.

*Jim Cymbala*

Wait on the LORD: be of good courage,
and he shall strengthen thine heart:
wait, I say, on the LORD.

*Psalm 27:14 KJV*

Heavenly Father, let me wait quietly for You.
May I live according to Your plan and according to
Your timetable. When I am hurried, slow me
down. When I become impatient with others, give
me empathy. Today, let me be a patient Christian
as I trust in You, Father, and in Your master plan.
—Amen—

# PEACE

Peace I leave with you, my peace I give unto you:
not as the world giveth, give I unto you. Let not
your heart be troubled, neither let it be afraid.

*John 14:27 KJV*

Have you found the genuine peace that can
be yours through Jesus Christ? Or are you
still rushing after the illusion of "peace and
happiness" that the world promises but cannot
deliver? The beautiful words of John 14:27 remind
us that Jesus offers us peace, not as the world gives,
but as He alone gives. Our challenge is to accept
Christ's peace into our hearts and then, as best we
can, to share His peace with our neighbors.

Today, as a gift to yourself, to your family, and to
your friends, claim the inner peace that is your
spiritual birthright: the peace of Jesus Christ. It is
offered freely; it has been paid for in full; it is yours
for the asking. So ask. And then share.

The more closely you cling to the Lord Jesus,
the more clear will your peace be.

*C. H. Spurgeon*

# GOD'S PEACE

The next time the demands of the day leave
you stressed, remember the peace of God that
comes through Christ Jesus. Open your heart
to Him, and He will give you a peace that
endures forever: His peace.

*Jim Gallery*


The peace that Jesus gives is never engineered
by circumstances on the outside.

*Oswald Chambers*


Come unto me, all ye that labor and are
heavy laden, and I will give you rest.

*Matthew 11:28 KJV*

Dear Lord, the peace that the world offers
is fleeting, but You offer a peace that is perfect
and eternal. Let me turn the cares and burdens of
my life over to You, Father, and let me feel
the spiritual abundance that You offer through
the person of Your Son, the Prince of Peace.

—Amen—

# POSSESSIONS

A man's life does not consist in
the abundance of his possessions.

*Luke 12:15 NIV*

How important are material possessions? Not as important as you might think. In the life of a committed Christian, material possessions should play a rather small role. Of course, we all need the basic necessities of life, but once we meet those needs for ourselves and for our families, the piling up of possessions creates more problems than it solves. Our real riches, of course, are not of this world. We are never really rich until we are rich in spirit.

Do you find yourself wrapped up in the concerns of the material world? If so, it's time to reorder your priorities by turning your thoughts and your prayers to more important matters. And, it's time to begin storing up riches that will endure throughout eternity: the spiritual kind.

Hold everything earthly with a loose hand,
but grasp eternal things with a deathlike grip.

*C. H. Spurgeon*

# THE TRAP OF MATERIALISM

It is not wrong to own things,
but it is wrong for things to own us.

*Warren Wiersbe*

When possessions become our god, we become
materialistic and greedy…and we forfeit
our contentment and our joy.

*Charles Swindoll*

Love not the world, neither the things that
are in the world. If any man love the world,
the love of the Father is not in him.

*1 John 2:15 KJV*

Lord, my greatest possession is my relationship
with You through Jesus Christ. You have promised
that, when I first seek Your kingdom and Your
righteousness, You will give me whatever I need.
Let me trust You completely, Lord, for my needs,
both material and spiritual, this day and always.

—Amen—

# PRAISE

From the rising of the sun to its setting,
the name of the LORD is to be praised.

*Psalm 113:3 NASB*

The psalmist writes, "Let everything that has breath praise the LORD. Praise the LORD!" (150:6 NASB). As Christians, we should continually praise God for all that He has done and all that He will do. For believers who have accepted the transforming love of Jesus Christ, there is simply no other way.

Today, as you travel to work or school, as you hug your child or kiss your spouse, as you gaze upon a passing cloud or marvel at a glorious sunset, think of what God has done for you, for yours, and for all of us. And, every time you notice a gift from the Giver of all things good, praise Him. His works are marvelous, His gifts are beyond understanding, and His love endures forever.

Praise reestablishes the proper chain of command;
we recognize that the King is on the throne and
that he has saved his people.

*Max Lucado*

# PRAISING GOD

The Bible instructs—and experience teaches—
that praising God results in our burdens being
lifted and our joys being multiplied.

*Jim Gallery*


When we come before the Lord with praise,
humbly repent of our transgressions,
and in obedience present our petitions to God
according to the guidelines set out for us
in Scripture, He will answer.

*Shirley Dobson*


I will praise thee with my whole heart....

*Psalm 138:1 KJV*


Heavenly Father, Your gifts are greater than
I can imagine, and Your love for me is greater
than I can fathom. May I live each day with
thanksgiving in my heart and praise on my lips.
Thank You for the gift of Your Son and for the
promise of eternal life. Let me share the joyous
news of Jesus Christ with a world that needs
His healing touch this day and every day.

—Amen—

# PRAYER

Rejoice evermore. Pray without ceasing.
In every thing give thanks: for this is the will of
God in Christ Jesus concerning you.

*1 Thessalonians 5:16-18 KJV*

I s prayer an integral part of your daily life or is it a hit-or-miss habit? Do you "pray without ceasing," or is your prayer life an afterthought? Do you regularly pray in the solitude of the early morning darkness, or do you bow your head only when others are watching?

The quality of your spiritual life will be in direct proportion to the quality of your prayer life. Prayer changes things, and it changes you. Today, instead of turning things over in your mind, turn them over to God in prayer. Instead of worrying about your next decision, ask God to lead the way. Don't limit your prayers to meals or to bedtime. Pray constantly about things great and small. God is listening, and He wants to hear from you.

If the spiritual life is to be healthy and under
the full power of the Holy Spirit,
praying without ceasing will be natural.

*Andrew Murray*

# THE POWER OF PRAYER

True prayer is measured by weight, not by length.
A single groan before God may have more fullness
of prayer in it than a fine oration of great length.

*C. H. Spurgeon*

God shapes the world by prayer. The more praying
there is in the world, the better the world will be,
and the mightier will be the forces against evil.

*E. M. Bounds*

Is anyone among you suffering?
Then he must pray.

*James 5:13 NASB*

Dear Lord, Your Holy Word commands me to pray
without ceasing. Let me take everything to You in
prayer. When I am discouraged, let me pray. When
I am lonely, let me take my sorrows to You. When
I grieve, let me take my tears to You, Lord, in
prayer. And when I am joyful, let me offer up
prayers of thanksgiving. In all things great and
small, at all times, whether happy or sad, let me
seek Your wisdom and Your Grace…in prayer.

—Amen—

# PRIDE

Pride goes before destruction,
a haughty spirit before a fall.

*Proverbs 16:18 NIV*

The words from Proverbs 16 remind us that pride and destruction usually travel arm in arm. But as imperfect human beings, we are tempted to puff our chests and crow about our own accomplishments. When we do so, we delude ourselves.

As Christians, we have a profound reason to be humble: we have been refashioned and saved by Jesus Christ, and that salvation came not because of our own good works but because of God's grace. Thus, we are not "self-made"; we are "God-made" and "Christ-saved." How, then, can we be boastful? The answer, of course, is simple: if we are honest with ourselves and with our God, we cannot be boastful. In the quiet moments, when we search the depths of our own hearts, we know that whatever "it" is, God did that. And He deserves the credit.

Humility is a thing which must be genuine;
the imitation of it is the nearest thing
in the world to pride.

*C. H. Spurgeon*

# The Pitfalls of Pride

The Lord sends no one away empty except
those who are full of themselves.

*D. L. Moody*

Let your old age be childlike, and childhood like
old age; that is, so that neither may your wisdom
be with pride, nor your humility without wisdom.

*St. Augustine*

A man's pride shall bring him low:
but honor shall uphold the humble in spirit.

*Proverbs 29:23 KJV*

Heavenly Father, it is the nature of mankind to
be prideful, and I am no exception. When I am
boastful, Lord, keep me mindful that all my gifts
come from You. When I feel prideful, remind me
that You sent Your Son to be a humble carpenter
and that Jesus was ridiculed and crucified on
a cross. Let me look only to You for approval.
You are the Giver of all things good;
let me give all the glory to You.

—Amen—

# RIGHTEOUSNESS

Walk in a manner worthy of the God who calls
you into His own kingdom and glory.
*1 Thessalonians 2:12 NASB*

The author of My *Utmost for His Highest*,
Oswald Chambers, advised, "Never support
an experience which does not have God as its source,
and faith in God as its result." These words serve as
a powerful reminder that, as Christians, we are called
to walk with God and obey His commandments. But,
we live in a world that presents us with countless
temptations to stray far from God's path. We
Christians, when confronted with sin, have clear
instructions: walk—or better yet run—in the
opposite direction.

Today, take every step of your journey with God
as your traveling companion. Read His Word and
follow His commandments. Support only those
activities that further God's kingdom and your
spiritual growth. Be an example of righteous living
to your friends, to your neighbors, and to your
children. Then, reap the blessings that God has
promised to all those who live according to His will
and His Word.

# LIVING RIGHTEOUSLY

A life growing in its purity and devotion
will be a more prayerful life.
*E. M. Bounds*

It may be said without qualification that every
man is as holy and as full of the Spirit as he wants
to be. He may not be as full as he wishes he were,
but he is most certainly as full as he wants to be.
*A. W. Tozer*

Blessed are those who hunger and thirst for
righteousness, for they will be filled.
*Matthew 5:6 NIV*

Lord, this world is filled with temptations,
distractions, and frustrations. But when I trust in
Your commandments and turn my prayers to You,
I am safe. Direct my path far from the temptations
and distractions of the world. Let me discover Your
will and follow it, Father, this day and always.
—Amen—

# SALVATION

For God so loved the world, that he gave his only
begotten Son, that whosoever believeth in him
should not perish, but have everlasting life.

*John 3:16 KJV*

Christ sacrificed His life on the cross so that
we might have eternal life. This gift, freely
given by God's only begotten Son, is the priceless
possession of everyone who accepts Him as Lord and
Savior. God is waiting patiently for each of us to
accept the gift of eternal life. Let us claim Christ's
gift today.

It is by God's grace that we have been saved,
through faith. We are saved not because of our good
deeds but because of our faith in Christ. May we,
who have been given so much, praise our Savior for
the gift of salvation, and may we share the joyous
news of our Master's love and His grace.

There is no one so far lost that Jesus cannot find
him and cannot save him.

*Andrew Murray*

# The Gift of Salvation

God is always ready to meet people wherever they are, no matter how dreadful their sins may seem.

*Jim Cymbala*

Salvation is the process that's done, that's secure, that no one can take away from you. Sanctification is the lifelong process of being changed from one degree of glory to the next, growing in Christ, putting away the old, taking on the new.

*Max Lucado*

I assure you: Anyone who believes has eternal life.

*John 6:47 HCSB*

+=====+

Lord, I am only here on this earth for a brief while. But, You have offered me the priceless gift of eternal life through Your Son Jesus. I accept Your gift, Lord, with thanksgiving and praise. Let me share the good news of my salvation with those who need Your healing touch.

—Amen—

# SEEKING GOD

The LORD is with you when you are with him.
If you seek him, he will be found by you,
but if you forsake him, he will forsake you.

*2 Chronicles 15:2 NIV*

Where is God? He is everywhere you have ever been and everywhere you will ever go. He is with you night and day; He knows your every thought; He hears your every heartbeat.

Sometimes, in the crush of your daily duties, God may seem far away. Or sometimes, when the disappointments and sorrows of life leave you breathless, God may seem distant, but He is not. When you earnestly seek God, you will find Him because He is here, waiting patiently for you to reach out to Him . . . right here . . . right now.

The key to a blessed life is to have a listening heart that longs to know what the Lord is saying.

*Jim Cymbala*

# In the Presence of God

O God. You are always the same.
Let me know myself and know You.

*St. Augustine*


Fix your eyes upon the Lord! Do it once.
Do it daily. Do it constantly. Look at the Lord
and keep looking at Him.

*Charles Swindoll*


But if from there you seek the LORD your God, you
will find him if you look for him with
all your heart and with all your soul.

*Deuteronomy 4:29 NIV*

How comforting it is, Dear Lord, to know that if
I seek You, I will find You. You are with me,
Father, every step that I take. Let me reach out
to You, and let me praise You for revealing
Your Word, Your way, and Your love.

—Amen—

# SERVICE

But a Samaritan, as he traveled,
came where the man was; and when he saw him,
he took pity on him. He went to him and
bandaged his wounds, pouring on oil and wine.
Then he put the man on his own donkey, took
him to an inn and took care of him.

*Luke 10:33-34 NIV*

The teachings of Jesus are crystal clear: we achieve greatness through service to others. But, as weak human beings, we sometimes fall short as we seek to puff ourselves up and glorify our own accomplishments. Jesus commands otherwise. He teaches us that the most esteemed men and women are not the self-congratulatory leaders of society but are instead the humblest of servants.

As a humble servant, you will glorify yourself not before men, but before God, and that's what God intends. After all, earthly glory is fleeting: here today and all too soon gone. But, heavenly glory endures throughout eternity. So, the choice is yours: Either you can lift yourself up here on earth and be humbled in heaven, or vice versa. Choose vice versa.

Holy service in constant fellowship
with God is heaven below.

*C. H. Spurgeon*

# SERVING OTHERS

There are times when we are called to love,
expecting nothing in return. There are times when
we are called to give money to people who
will never say thanks, to forgive those who
won't forgive us, to come early and stay late
when no one else notices.

*Max Lucado*


Have thy tools ready; God will find thee work.

*Charles Kingsley*


Each of you should look not only to your own
interests, but also to the interest of others.

*Philippians 2:4 NIV*


Dear Lord, in weak moments, I seek to build
myself up by placing myself ahead of others.
But Your commandment, Father, is that I become
a humble servant to those who need my
encouragement, my help, and my love. Create
in me a servant's heart. And, let me follow in
the footsteps of Your Son Jesus, who taught us by
example that to be great in Your eyes, Lord,
is to serve others humbly, faithfully, and lovingly.
—Amen—

# STRENGTH

I am able to do all things through Him
who strengthens me.

*Philippians 4:13 HCSB*

God is a never-ending source of strength and
courage if we call upon Him. When we
are weary, He gives us strength. When we see no
hope, God reminds us of His promises. When we
grieve, God wipes away our tears.

Do you feel overwhelmed by today's responsibilities? Do you feel pressured by the ever-increasing
demands of 21st-century life? Then turn your
concerns and your prayers over to God. He knows
your needs, and He has promised to meet those needs.
Whatever your circumstances, God will protect you
and care for you…if you let Him. Invite Him into
your heart and allow Him to renew your spirit. When
you trust Him and Him alone, He will never fail you.

We are never stronger than
the moment we admit we are weak.

*Beth Moore*

# Finding Strength through God

God conquers only what we yield to Him.
Yet, when He does, and when our surrender is
complete, He fills us with a new strength that we
could never have known by ourselves.
His conquest is our victory!

*Shirley Dobson*


If we take God's program, we can have
God's power—not otherwise.

*E. Stanley Jones*


He said unto me, My grace is sufficient for thee:
for my strength is made perfect in weakness.

*2 Corinthians 12:9 KJV*


Lord, sometimes life is difficult. Sometimes,
I am worried, weary, or heartbroken. But, when
I lift my eyes to You, Father, You strengthen me.
When I am weak, You lift me up. Today,
I turn to You, Lord, for my strength, for my hope,
and my salvation.

—Amen—

# SUCCESS

Success, success to you, and success to those who
help you, for your God will help you....

*1 Chronicles 12:18 NIV*

How do you define success? Do you define it as the accumulation of material possessions or the adulation of your neighbors? If so, you need to reorder your priorities. Genuine success has little to do with fame or fortune; it has everything to do with God's gift of love and His promise of salvation.

If you have accepted Christ as your personal savior, you are already a towering success in the eyes of God, but there is still more that you can do. Your task—as a believer who has been touched by the Creator's grace—is to accept the spiritual abundance and peace that He offers through the person of His Son. Then, you can share the healing message of God's love and His abundance with a world that desperately needs both. When you do, you have reached the pinnacle of success.

Never forget: If you belong to the King,
you are on the winning side.

*Billy Graham*

# Thoughts on Successful Living

We, as believers, must allow God to define success.
And, when we do, God blesses us with
His love and His grace.

*Jim Gallery*


Success and happiness are not destinations.
They are exciting, never-ending journeys.

*Zig Ziglar*


Have faith in the LORD your God and
you will be upheld; have faith in his prophets
and you will be successful.

*2 Chronicles 20:20 NIV*

Dear Lord, let me define success not according
to the world's standards but according to Yours.
Let me seek approval not from fallible men
and women, but from You.

—Amen—

# TALENT

Do not neglect the spiritual gift
that is within you….

*1 Timothy 4:14 NASB*

The old saying is both familiar and true: "What we are is God's gift to us; what we become is our gift to God." Each of us possesses special talents, gifted by God, that can be nurtured carefully or ignored totally. Our challenge, of course, is to use our abilities to the greatest extent possible and to use them in ways that honor our Savior.

Are you using your natural talents to make God's world a better place? If so, congratulations. But if you have gifts that you have not fully explored and developed, perhaps you need to have a chat with the One who gave you those gifts in the first place. Your talents are priceless treasures offered from your Heavenly Father. Use them. After all, an obvious way to say "thank you" to the Giver is to use the gifts He has given.

Natural abilities are like natural plants;
they need pruning by study.

*Francis Bacon*

# Using Your Talents

In the great orchestra we call life, you have
an instrument and a song, and you owe it
to God to play them both sublimely.

*Max Lucado*

Employ whatever God has entrusted you with,
in doing good, all possible good,
in every possible kind and degree.

*John Wesley*

I remind you to keep ablaze the gift of God
that is in you....

*2 Timothy 1:6 HCSB*

Lord, You gave me talents and abilities for a
reason. Let me use my talents for the glory of Your
kingdom, and let me praise You always because
You are the Giver of all gifts, including mine.
—Amen—

# TEMPTATION

Put on the whole armour of God, that ye may be
able to stand against the wiles of the devil.

*Ephesians 6:11 KJV*

How hard is it to bump into temptation in
this crazy world? Not very hard. The devil,
it seems, is working overtime these days while causing
pain and heartache in more places and in more ways
than ever before. We, as Christians, must remain
vigilant. Not only must we resist Satan when he
confronts us, but we must also avoid those places
where Satan can most easily tempt us.

When we are confronted with the temptations
of an iniquitous world, we must earnestly wrap
ourselves in the protection of God's Holy Word.
When we do, we are secure.

In the worst temptations nothing can help us but
faith that God's Son has put on flesh, sits at
the right hand of the Father, and prays for us.
There is no mightier comfort.

*Martin Luther*

# Turning Away from Temptation

No trial is too great, no temptation is too strong,
but that Jesus Christ can give us the mercy and
the grace that we need, when we need it.

*Warren Wiersbe*

Since you are tempted without ceasing,
pray without ceasing.

*C. H. Spurgeon*

No temptation has seized you except what is
common to man. And God is faithful; he will not
let you be tempted beyond what you can bear.
But when you are tempted, he will also provide
a way out so that you can stand up under it.

*1 Corinthians 10:13 NIV*

+≈≈+

Lord, life is filled with temptations to stray from
Your chosen path. But, I face no temptation that
You have not already met and conquered through
my Lord and Savior Jesus Christ, the One who
empowers me with His strength and His love.

—Amen—

# TESTIMONY

Also I say unto you, Whosoever shall confess
me before men, him shall the Son of man also
confess before the angels of God: but he that
denieth me before men shall be denied
before the angels of God.

*Luke 12:8-9 KJV*

In his second letter to Timothy, Paul shares a
message to believers of every generation when
he writes, "God has not given us a spirit of timidity"
(1:7 NASB). Paul's meaning is crystal clear: when
sharing our testimonies, we, as Christians, must be
courageous, forthright, and unashamed.

We live in a world that desperately needs the
healing message of Christ Jesus. Every believer, each
in his or her own way, bears a personal responsibility
for sharing that message. If you are a believer in
Christ, you know how He has touched your heart
and changed your life. Now it's your turn to share
the good news with others. And remember: today is
the perfect time to share your testimony because
tomorrow may be too late.

Our faith grows by expression. If we want to keep
our faith, we must share it. We must act.

*Billy Graham*

# SHARING YOUR TESTIMONY

Remember, a small light will do a great deal when
it is in a very dark place. Put one little tallow
candle in the middle of a large hall, and
it will give a great deal of light.

*D. L. Moody*

Jesus made Himself known to His own, and
if others are to hear about him today, you and
I must tell them.

*Vance Havner*

You are a chosen people. You are a kingdom of
priests, God's holy nation, his very own possession.
This is so you can show others the goodness of
God, for he called you out of the darkness
into his wonderful light.

*1 Peter 2:9 NLT*

Lord, You have saved me through the gift of Your
Son. Let me share the story of my salvation with
others so that they, too, might dedicate their lives
to Jesus and receive His eternal gifts.

—Amen—

# THANKSGIVING

Give thanks in all circumstances;
for this is God's will for you in Christ Jesus.
*1 Thessalonians 5:18 NIV*

The words of 1 Thessalonians 5:18 remind us to give thanks in every circumstance of life. But sometimes, when our hearts are troubled and our spirits are crushed, we don't feel like celebrating. Yet even when the clouds of despair darken our lives, God offers us His love, His strength, and His grace. And as believers, we must thank Him.

Have you thanked God today for blessings that are too numerous to count? Have you offered Him your heartfelt prayers and your wholehearted praise? If not, it's time to slow down and to offer a prayer of thanksgiving to the One who has given you life on earth and life eternal.

No matter our circumstances, we owe God so much more than we can ever repay, and the least we can do is to thank Him.

The words "thank" and "think" come from
the same root word. If we would think more,
we would thank more.
*Warren Wiersbe*

# GIVING THANKS TO GOD

We ought to give thanks for all fortune: if it is
good, because it is good; if bad, because it works in
us patience, humility, and the contempt of this
world along with the hope of our eternal country.

*C. S. Lewis*


Why wait until the fourth Thursday in November?
Why wait until the morning of December 25th?
Thanksgiving to God should be an everyday affair.
The time to be thankful is now!

*Jim Gallery*


Thanks be to God for His indescribable gift.

*2 Corinthians 9:15 HCSB*

+===+

Heavenly Father, Your gifts are greater than
I can imagine. May I live each day with
thanksgiving in my heart and praise on my lips.
Thank You for the gift of Your Son and for the
promise of eternal life. Let me share the joyous
news of Jesus Christ, and let my life be
a testimony to His love and His grace.
—Amen—

# TODAY

This is the day which the LORD hath made;
we will rejoice and be glad in it.

*Psalm 118:24 KJV*

For Christian believers, every day begins and ends with God and His Son. Christ came to this earth to give us abundant life and eternal salvation. Our task is to accept Christ's grace with joy in our hearts and praise on our lips. Believers who fashion their days around Jesus are transformed: they see the world differently, they act differently, and they feel differently about themselves and their neighbors.

The familiar words of Psalm 118:24 remind us that every day is a gift from God. So whatever this day holds for you, begin it and end it with God as your partner and Christ as your Savior. And throughout the day, give thanks to the One who created you and saved you. God's love for you is infinite. Accept it joyously and be thankful.

Submit each day to God, knowing that
He is God over all your tomorrows.

*Kay Arthur*

# CELEBRATING THIS DAY!

A man can no more take in a supply of grace
for the future than he can eat enough for the next
six months, or take sufficient air into his lungs
at one time to sustain life for a week. We must
draw upon God's boundless store of grace from
day to day as we need it.

*D. L. Moody*

I will give thanks to the LORD with all my heart;
I will tell of all Your wonders. I will be glad and
exult in You; I will sing praise to Your name,
O Most High.

*Psalm 9:1-2 NASB*

Lord, You have given me another day of life;
let me celebrate this day, and let me use it
according to Your plan. I praise You, Father,
for my life and for the friends and family members
who make it rich. Enable me to live each moment
to the fullest as I give thanks for Your creation,
for Your love, and for Your Son.

—Amen—

# TRUSTING GOD

The LORD's unfailing love surrounds
the man who trusts in him.

*Psalm 32:10 NIV*

The journey through life leads us over many peaks and through many valleys. When we reach the mountaintops, we find it easy to praise God, to trust Him, and to give thanks. But, when we trudge through the dark valleys of bitterness and despair, trusting God is more difficult.

The next time you find your courage tested to the limit, lean upon God's promises. Trust His Son. When you are worried, anxious, or afraid, call upon Him. God can handle your troubles infinitely better than you can, so turn them over to Him. Remember that God rules both mountaintops and valleys—with limitless wisdom and love—now and forever.

Trust in yourself and you are doomed to
disappointment; trust in money and you may have
it taken from you, but trust in God, and you are
never to be confounded in time or eternity.

*D. L. Moody*

# TRUSTING THE FATHER

God has proven himself as a faithful father.
Now it falls to us to be trusting children.

*Max Lucado*

You will be able to trust Him only to the extent
that you know Him!

*Kay Arthur*

Trust the past to God's mercy, the present to
God's love, and the future to God's providence.

*St. Augustine*

O LORD of hosts, blessed is the man
that trusteth in thee.

*Psalm 84:12 KJV*

＋≈＋

Today, Lord, I will trust You and seek Your will
for my life. You have a plan for me, Father.
Let me discover it and live it, knowing that when
I trust in You, I am eternally blessed.

—Amen—

# TRUSTWORTHINESS

Walk in a manner worthy of the God who calls
you into His own kingdom and glory.
*1 Thessalonians 2:12 NASB*

Do you intend to do your best to be a righteous man in the eyes of God? If so, you must make every effort to be a man of integrity.

Character is built slowly over a lifetime. It is the sum of every right decision, every honest word, every noble thought, and every heartfelt prayer. It is forged on the anvil of honorable work and polished by the twin virtues of generosity and humility. Character is a precious thing—difficult to build but easy to tear down. As believers in Christ, we must seek to live each day with discipline, honesty, and faith. When we do, integrity becomes a habit.

Today and every day, vow to be a man whose behavior is worthy of the One who has saved You. Your friends and family members deserve no less . . . and neither does your Savior.

Integrity is the glue that holds our way of life together. We must constantly strive to keep our integrity intact. When wealth is lost, nothing is lost; when health is lost, something is lost; when character is lost, all is lost.

*Billy Graham*

# A TRUSTWORTHY MAN

Impurity is not just a wrong action; impurity is
the state of mind and heart and soul which is just
the opposite of purity and wholeness.

*A. W. Tozer*

Nothing speaks louder or more powerfully
than a life of integrity.

*Charles Swindoll*

Be thou an example of the believers, in word,
in conversation, in charity, in spirit,
in faith, in purity.

*1 Timothy 4:12 KJV*

Dear Lord, make me a man who is worthy
of others' trust. Let me seek the truth and speak
the truth, today and every day of my life. May
Jesus always be the standard for truth in my life
so that I might be a worthy example to others
and a worthy servant to You.

—Amen—

# WISDOM

Choose my instruction instead of silver,
knowledge rather than choice gold, for wisdom
is more precious than rubies, and nothing
you desire can compare with her.

*Proverbs 8:10-11 NIV*

S ometimes, amid the demands of daily life,
we lose perspective. Life seems out of
balance, and the pressures of everyday living seem
overwhelming. What's needed is a fresh perspective,
a restored sense of balance…and God's wisdom.

If we call upon the Lord and seek to see the world
through His eyes, He will give us guidance, wisdom,
and perspective. When we make God's priorities our
priorities, He will lead us according to His plan and
according to His commandments. When we study
God's Word, we are reminded that God's reality is
the ultimate reality. May we live accordingly.

The doorstep to the temple of wisdom
is a knowledge of our own ignorance.

*C. H. Spurgeon*

# God's Wisdom

If you lack knowledge, go to school.
If you lack wisdom, get on your knees.
*Vance Havner*

When you persevere through a trial, God gives
you a special measure of insight.
*Charles Swindoll*

I will instruct you and teach you in the way you
should go; I will counsel you and watch over you.
*Psalm 32:8 NIV*

+‗‗‗+

I seek wisdom, Dear Father, not as the world gives,
but as You give. Lead me in Your ways and teach
me from Your Word so that, in time, my wisdom
might glorify Your kingdom, Lord, and Your Son.
—Amen—

# WORRY

So do not worry, saying, "What shall we eat?" or
"What shall we drink?" or "What shall we wear?"
For the pagans run after all these things, and your
heavenly Father knows that you need them. But
seek first his kingdom and his righteousness, and
all these things will be given to you as well.
Therefore do not worry about tomorrow,
for tomorrow will worry about itself. Each day
has enough trouble of its own.

*Matthew 6:31-34 NIV*

If you are a man with lots of obligations and
plenty of responsibilities, it is simply a fact
of life: you worry. From time to time, you worry about
health, about finances, about safety, about family,
and about countless other concerns, some great and
some small.

Where is the best place to take your worries?
Take them to God. Take your troubles to Him; take
your fears to Him; take your doubts to Him; take
your weaknesses to Him; take your sorrows to Him…
and leave them all there. Seek protection with the
One who offers you eternal salvation; build your
spiritual house upon the Rock that cannot be moved.

Worry makes you forget who's in charge.

*Max Lucado*

# Thoughts on the Futility of Worry

The secret of Christian quietness is not
indifference, but the knowledge that God is my
Father, He loves me, and that I shall never
think of anything that He will forget.
Then, worry becomes an impossibility.

*Oswald Chambers*

Be anxious for nothing, but in everything by
prayer and supplication with thanksgiving let
your requests be made known to God.

*Philippians 4:6 NASB*

Lord, You sent Your Son to live as a man on
this earth, and You know what it means to be
completely human. You understand my worries
and fears, Lord, and You forgive me when I am
weak. When my faith begins to wane, help me,
Lord, to trust You more. Then, with Your Holy
Word on my lips and with the love of Your Son in
my heart, let me live courageously, faithfully,
prayerfully, and thankfully today and every day.

—Amen—

# WORSHIP

I was glad when they said unto me,
Let us go into the house of the LORD.

*Psalm 122:1 KJV*

All of mankind is engaged in the practice of worship. Some people choose to worship God and, as a result, reap the joy that He intends for His children. Others distance themselves from God by worshiping such things as earthly possessions or personal gratification…and when they do, they suffer.

What will you choose to worship today? Will you worship your Creator or your possessions? Will you worship your Savior, Jesus Christ, or will you bow down before the false gods of pride and avarice? Will you seek the approval of your God or the approval of your neighbors? Every day provides opportunities to put God where He belongs: at the center of your life. Worship Him—and only Him—today, tomorrow, and always.

Worship is not taught from the pulpit.
It must be learned in the heart.

*Jim Elliot*

# WORSHIPING THE CREATOR

In the sanctuary, we discover beauty:
the beauty of His presence.
*Kay Arthur*


Inside the human heart is an undeniable,
spiritual instinct to commune with its Creator.
*Jim Cymbala*


All the earth shall worship thee, and shall sing
unto thee; and shall sing to thy name....
*Psalm 66:4 KJV*


When I worship You, Lord, You direct my path
and You cleanse my heart. Let today and every day
be a time of worship and praise. Let me worship
You in everything that I think and do. Thank You,
Lord, for the priceless gift of Your Son Jesus.
Let me be worthy of that gift, and let me give
You the praise and the glory forever.
—Amen—